Hansel
and Gretel and the
Witch's Cat

by Damian Harvey and Pauline Gregory

W

FRANKLIN WATTS

LONDON · SYDNEY

Hansel and Gretel lived in a small cottage with their father and stepmother. They were very poor.

One day, there was no wood left for the fire.

"You must go into the forest to find some firewood," said their father.

Hansel and Gretel took some bread to eat and off they went.

Hansel and Gretel did not like
the big, dark forest.

"We might get lost," said Hansel.

"We will not get lost," said Gretel.

"We can drop breadcrumbs
to show us the way home."

Hansel and Gretel soon collected
lots of firewood. But when it was time
to go home, they could not find
the breadcrumbs.
"The birds have eaten them,"
said Gretel.

Hansel and Gretel walked deeper into the forest.
After a long time, they came to a small cottage.
"It is made of cake and sweets," said Hansel.

Gretel ran up to the cottage and broke off a piece of the windowsill. "Yum!" she cried, and she started to eat.

Just then, the cottage door opened,
and an old woman came out.

"Come in, come in," she said, smiling.

"I have lots more sweets inside."

Hansel and Gretel were very hungry,
so they went inside.
The old woman closed the door.

The old woman was not smiling now.

She pushed Hansel into a cage and

locked the door.

"'I am going to give you lots to eat,

so you get nice and fat.

Then I will eat you," she laughed.

"She must be a witch," cried Gretel.

The witch looked at Gretel.

"You will clean my house," she said.

The witch made Gretel
clean the house while
she counted her gold coins.

The witch peered at Hansel. "I cannot see you," she said. "Are you fat enough to eat yet? Let me feel your finger." Quickly, the witch's cat gave Hansel a chicken bone and Hansel held it out for the witch to feel.

"Too thin!" cried the witch.

The next day, the witch was
too hungry to wait any longer.
"I'll eat him today!" she yelled,
and she lit the oven.
After a while, she told Gretel to get
inside to see if it was hot enough.

"Say that you are too big to fit inside," the cat told Gretel.

Gretel did what the cat had told her.

The witch was angry.

"The oven is big," she said.

"Even I can fit inside."

She opened the oven door.

"Quick," said the cat. "Push her in."
Gretel did what the cat had told her
and pushed the witch into the oven.
The cat slammed the oven door.
Gretel let Hansel out of the cage.

"We must run home," said Gretel.

"But we don't know the way," said Hansel.

"I will show you," said the cat.

"Bring the gold with you."

When they got home, their father and stepmother were so happy to see them.

"You are safe," said their father.

"Thanks to the witch's cat," said Gretel.

"And we have lots of gold," said Hansel.

"That's just what we needed," said their father.

And they all lived
happily ever after.

Story order

Look at these 5 pictures and captions.
Put the pictures in the right order
to retell the story.

1

The witch pushed Hansel into a cage.

2

They found a cottage made of sweets.

3

They came home with the witch's gold.

4

Hansel and Gretel got lost in the forest.

5

The witch was pushed into the oven.

Independent Reading

This series is designed to provide an opportunity for your child to read on their own. These notes are written for you to help your child choose a book and to read it independently.

In school, your child's teacher will often be using reading books which have been banded to support the process of learning to read. Use the book band colour your child is reading in school to help you make a good choice. *Hansel and Gretel and the Witch's Cat* is a good choice for children reading at Turquoise Band in their classroom to read independently.

The aim of independent reading is to read this book with ease, so that your child enjoys the story and relates it to their own experiences.

About the book
Hansel and Gretel find a cottage made of sweets, but a witch lives there, and she wants to eat Hansel! Luckily, the witch has a cat.

Before reading
Help your child to learn how to make good choices by asking: "Why did you choose this book? Why do you think you will enjoy it?" Look at the cover together and ask: "What do you think the story will be about?" Support your child to think of what they already know about the story context. Read the title aloud and ask: "Do you think the cottage on the cover looks like a nice place?" Remind your child that they can try to sound out the letters to make a word if they get stuck.

Decide together whether your child will read the story independently or read it aloud to you.

During reading

If reading aloud, support your child if they hesitate or ask for help by telling them the word. Remind your child of what they know and what they can do independently. If reading to themselves, remind your child that they can come and ask for your help if stuck.

After reading

Support comprehension by asking your child to tell you about the story. Use the story order puzzle to encourage your child to retell the story in the right sequence, in their own words. The correct sequence can be found on the next page.
Give your child a chance to respond to the story: "Did you have a favourite part? Did you expect the cat to help?"
Help your child think about the messages in the book that go beyond the story and ask: "What did Hansel and Gretel do wrong? How do they feel when they get home at the end?"

Extending learning

Think about the story with your child, and make comparisons with the story Hansel and Gretel, if this story is known to them. Help your child understand the story structure by using the same story context and adding different elements.
"Let's make up a new story about a witch's cottage. What happens in your story?"
In the classroom, your child's teacher may be reinforcing punctuation. On a few of the pages, ask your child to find the speech marks that show us where someone is talking and then read it aloud, making it sound like talking. Find the exclamation marks and ask your child to practise the expression they use for these.

Franklin Watts
First published in Great Britain in 2024
by Hodder and Stoughton
Copyright © Hodder and Stoughton, 2024

Series Editors: Jackie Hamley and Melanie Palmer
Series Advisors and Development Editors: Dr Sue Bodman
and Glen Franklin
Series Designers: Cathryn Gilbert and Peter Scoulding

A CIP catalogue record for this book is
available from the British Library.

ISBN 978 1 4451 8949 9 (hbk)
ISBN 978 1 4451 8951 2 (pbk)
ISBN 978 1 4451 8950 5 (ebook)

Printed in China

Franklin Watts
An imprint of
Hachette Children's Group
Part of Hodder and Stoughton
Carmelite House
50 Victoria Embankment
London EC4Y 0DZ

An Hachette UK Company
www.hachette.co.uk

www.reading-champion.co.uk

FSC
www.fsc.org
MIX
Paper | Supporting
responsible forestry
FSC® C104740

Story order: 4, 2, 1, 5, 3